This book
belongs to:

....

....

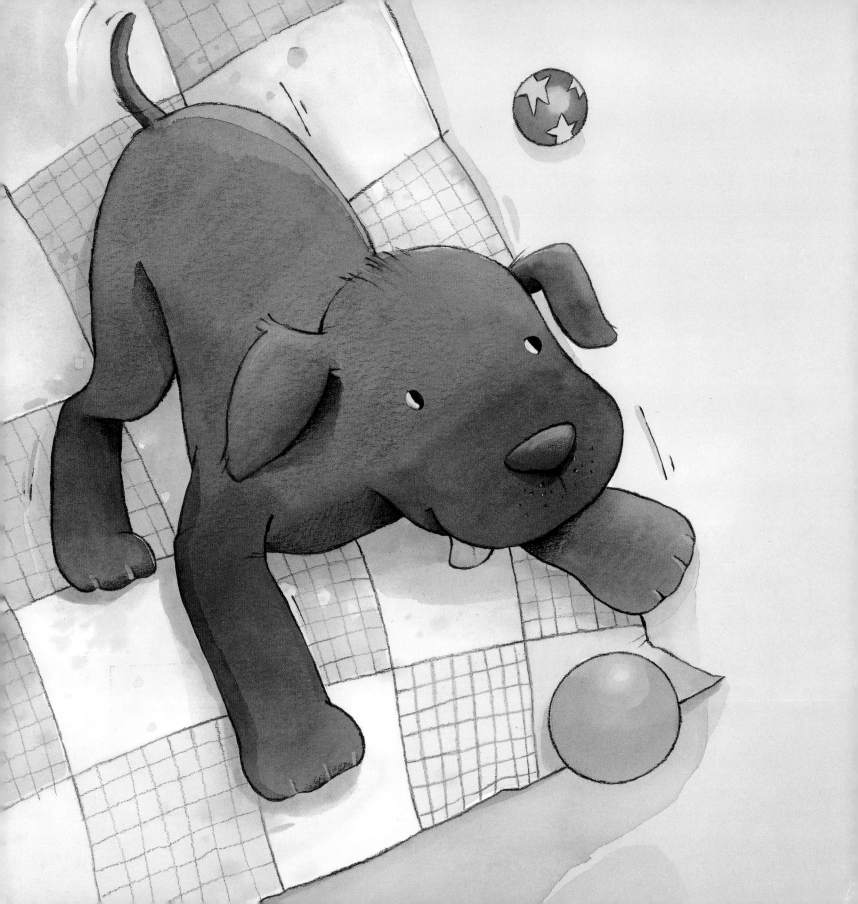

I Remember

Text: *Jennifer Moore-Mallinos*

Illustrations: *Marta Fàbrega*

BARRON'S

Did you know that we are born, we live,
and then one day we die?

Your pet also is born, lives, and dies. Life has a beginning and an end.

Do you have a pet now, or did
you have one before? What is
or was its name?

My pet's name was Jake. Jake was
the greatest dog in the whole world,
and he was my best friend.

I remember the first day I met Jake. He came running through our front door wearing a great big red bow around his neck. He ran straight toward me. I remember how excited he was when I picked him up to give him a hug. He was so wiggly, and his tail kept wagging!

He was the fluffiest puppy I had ever seen! Jake's circle of life began when he was born. As he grew and got older, the circle became more complete. Jake and I grew up together.

As Jake grew from a puppy into an adult dog, he went through many changes. Not only did he grow bigger, but every year he got a little older. As time went by, Jake's body became old and tired. He wasn't able to do the things he loved like chasing the chickens in the barn or running through the long grass in the field behind our house.

Jake's body was slowing down, and his eyes looked so sad. When we took Jake to see the animal doctor, called a veterinarian, he told my family that Jake was very sick and very old, and that he wasn't going to get better.

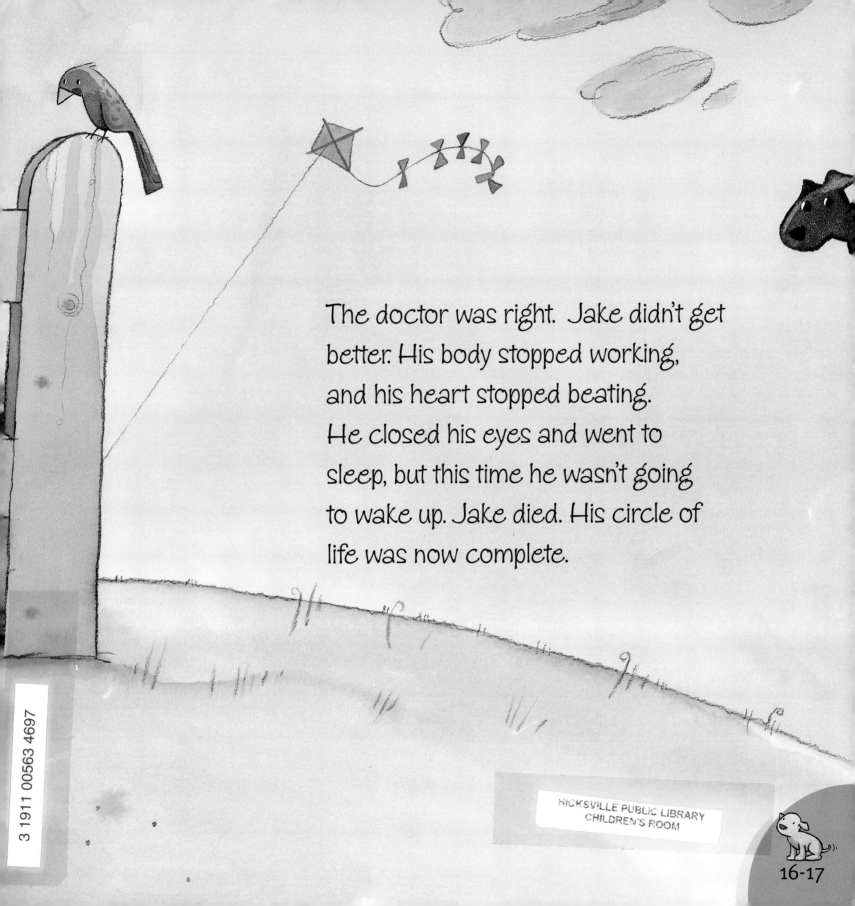

The doctor was right. Jake didn't get
better. His body stopped working,
and his heart stopped beating.
He closed his eyes and went to
sleep, but this time he wasn't going
to wake up. Jake died. His circle of
life was now complete.

I remember how sad and lonely I felt the day that Jake died. I couldn't stop crying, and I didn't feel like doing anything. My heart felt like it was going to break. What was I going to do without him? Part of me felt a little mad at Jake for leaving me because I thought best friends were supposed to be together forever. I felt better when my parents explained that Jake didn't have a choice about dying.

Jake was buried beneath the oak tree at the top of the hill that overlooked our farm. When we buried Jake, my family gathered around the oak tree to say good-bye. Saying good-bye to my best friend was really hard to do. I missed him so much. He had always been there for me.

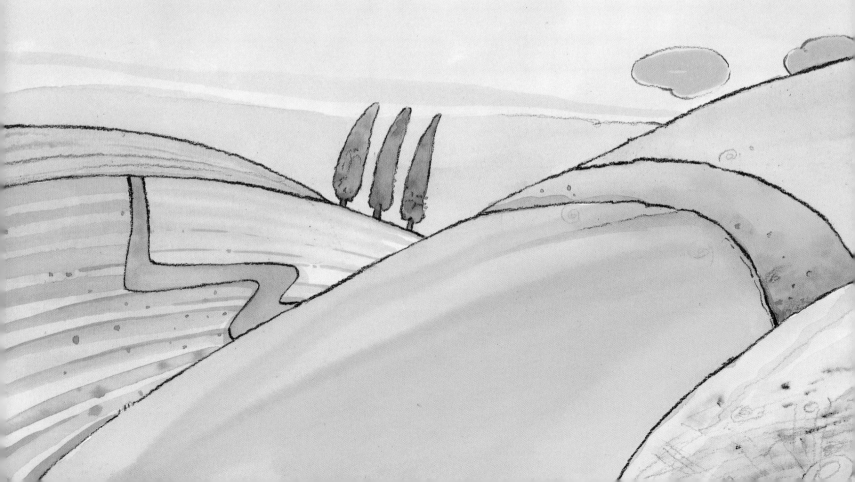

As time went by, I was able to remember all the
special things we did together without feeling so
sad. I remember how much fun we had playing hide
and seek in the barn, and how happy he was when
we went swimming at the lake. Jake really loved
swimming, and so did I.

Remembering Jake made me smile, and even though I couldn't see or touch him, he was always with me. I will always remember the time we spent together and how Jake taught me what it means to be a good friend. Sitting under that oak tree is still my favorite spot to go, especially on a hot day.

Today I met a new friend. His name is Lucas. He came running through our front door wearing a great big red bow around his neck, and he ran straight to me! When I picked him up to give him a hug, he squealed with delight. He was so cute!

Whenever I take Jake's picture out of my pocket, I know that Jake and Lucas would have become great friends, too! Even 'though I have a new friend, I will never forget Jake.
Jake will always be very special to me, no matter what!

Note to Parents

Pets come in all shapes and sizes, short or long hair, and different shades. No matter what kind of pet we have, they all possess distinct characteristics and personalities, and they all become an important part of the family.

I remember each one of my pets. Their loyalty, enthusiasm for life, and their unconditional friendship are things that I will treasure for the rest of my life. The bond I shared with each of my pets was unique and special, and the memories I have will always be with me.

We are born, we live, and then we die. The same happens with our pets. Life has a beginning and an end.

The purpose of this book is to acknowledge the friendship and love our children have for their pets and the overwhelming feelings of grief they may experience when the family pet dies.

The death of a pet is often our children's first experience with mortality. Such a traumatic event creates many feelings that may be difficult for them to understand. Validating your children's feelings by allowing them the opportunity to explore and express their grief is the first step in the process of healing.

I Remember can be used as a tool to initiate dialogue and stimulate communication between you and your child. Your child will be reminded that it is okay to feel sad or even mad when his or her best friend passes away.

I Remember also acknowledges that it's okay to love a new pet. The friendship and love we have shared with each of our pets will always be cherished and remembered, no matter what!

Taking the time to read to your child is a wonderful way to share a moment together. Let's do our part to show our children that we truly care!

I REMEMBER

First edition for the United States and Canada
published in 2005 by Barron's Educational Series, Inc.
© Copyright 2005 by Gemser Publications S.L.
C/Castell, 38; Teià (08329) Barcelona, Spain (World Rights)
Text: Jennifer Moore-Mallinos
Illustrations: Marta Fàbrega

Address all inquiries to:
Barron's Educational Series, Inc.
250 Wireless Boulevard
Hauppauge, New York 11788 USA
http://www.barronseduc.com

ISBN-13: 978-0-7641-3274-2
ISBN-10: 0-7641-3274-1
Library of Congress Control Card Number 2005926575

Printed in China
9 8 7 6 5 4 3 2 1